JOB SEARCH TIPS AND TECHNIQUES

A PRACTICAL GUIDE TO

FINDING A JOB

Ed Londergan

Award-winning author of *The Devil's Elbow*
and *The Long Journey Home*

To Van Leichter, the best of friends.

Introduction

Some sort of occupation or productive activity is necessary for human well-being. Without any activity, mental or physical, a person turns into a slug which is bad for both the person and society.

Conducting a job search and finding a job is not an easy task. It can be difficult, troubling, fear-inducing, and gut wrenching at times, but can also be rewarding and satisfying. I want to help guide you through that process based on my over thirty years of experience.

My qualifications on this topic are simple: I have been out of work three times in twelve years, managed various size groups of employees for many years and have been on the hiring side of the equation so I know what is involved in finding the best candidate. I have been a contractor and now have my own business. I will share with you all that I learned in my search for a great job and starting your own business.

Finding the courage to work for yourself and pursue a passion is possibly more difficult than securing a position with an employer for it takes a conviction that you can do what you are good at and do it well. However, to succeed you must prepare Grasshopper. We'll get into this in more detail later on.

As to the job search, we will cover the basics; there are many books that go into the details of each phase of the job search process. This one will give an overview of those activities you need to focus on to conclude a productive job search.

The job search process can be complicated as there are many interconnected factors. The best way is, like many things in life, to keep it simple. You have enough things on your plate and making the search process more complicated than it needs to be will cause you to waste valuable time and energy and may undermine a successful outcome.

As you begin your search, keep something in mind— this is a business action you are undertaking. It is not a social effort. Potential employers spend money, sometimes lots of money, to find a good candidate. You need to understand and accept that it is not a personal matter. If you do, you are well on your way. When you don't hear anything for weeks or get that rejection email, don't take it personally because it is not. It is a business matter pure and simple.

At certain times, it will seem like the search process will go on forever. That is not true unless you give up, which after many months of fruitless searching can be tempting. Just chuck it all, say the hell with it, and figure out how to live off of nothing. That is a mistake, a big mistake. Every time you feel that way, you need to grab yourselves by the bootstraps and pull yourself up. Some days you can't be bothered while on other days you'll go at it with gusto and enthusiasm. The thing to remember is that, no matter how hopeless things seem someone out there wants you to work for them; they just don't know it yet.

Everything I tell you will not be sunshine, rainbows, and lollipops. Much of it is difficult to hear and accept. It is a tough old world out there and you better be prepared to do all you can to get a good job, one that is right for you, or you will be sitting on the sidelines for a long time.

Be prepared to be frustrated and disappointed because it is going to happen. It is all part of the process and the sooner you recognize that the better off you will be. You will learn that not all positions are right for you, that not all employers make the best hiring decisions, that there is only so much you can do and then it is out of your hands. Yes, I know that is much easier said than done but it is true. If you do not get a job after great interviews you will wonder why. The old second guessing begins. What did I do wrong? What should I have done differently? The questions can go on forever. More than likely, you will never know why you weren't selected. What it comes down to is that they hired someone they thought was more qualified than you. Or better known to them—hiring from within or a better connected candidate. Not fun to hear but get over it. It is going to happen. Dealing with rejection is not an easy thing because we all take it personally when in fact, in the job hiring process; it is strictly a business decision not a popularity contest. The best advice I can impart is to forget it and move on to the next one.

You will get tired of looking. Getting the old "thanks but no thanks" over and over again is enough to discourage anyone but, to be successful, you must persevere. Piss and moan about how unfair it is, how wrong they are for not hiring you, and then get over it, and go find someone who values you for what you bring to them.

Another point to keep in mind is that the job search is a learning process, both of the things you need to do to be successful in securing a new position but also about you. In some ways, it is a journey of personal discovery. You will learn much if you are honest and genuine with yourself, something that is not always easy.

My first job search was a disaster because I did not know what I was doing and would not listen to anyone because I thought it could not be *that* difficult to find a job. That was a total misconception since I had not looked for a job in twenty years and had no idea how to go about it. My second search was better because I learned from the first search and made myself a student of the job search game. Since I am now in my late 50s, my third search was long and intense. This last job search, I found a job that was okay. While I did not really like the situation, it was a job. The work was interesting but the manager was not good and the commute, two hours a day, was just too much.

I met with a job coach to see if she could help me figure out what to do with my career. She opened my eyes by pointing out that I was ill-suited for my last several jobs because I wanted to do something else. She was correct — I wanted to write, edit, and teach writing but was afraid of failure so I never pursued it. One day shortly after meeting with her, I told my wife I wanted to write and edit and did not want to go back to my job. Her response: "Then don't." I informed my manager the next day and here I am.

One last thing to note is that these are my personal observations based on my experience. I am not a career coach, recruiter, or job placement counselor. Everything in this book is what I have learned over the years and resonated with me as a result of my searches.

PLANNING THE JOB SEARCH

To my way of thinking, the search process is composed of six activities: self-assessment, determination of your work desires and dreams, development of the appropriate resume and cover letters, networking, interviewing, and negotiation/acceptance of an offer.

Each of these activities is important and none should be disregarded because each one builds on another. Without knowing what you want, where to look, or how to look, you will never be able to find it. Simple but true.

Be careful not to rush into applying for jobs just so you can say you applied. Take a day or two or three and plan your search. One day, or even one week, will not make a huge difference at the beginning of your search. Take the time to get your ducks in order. Make sure you have everything covered before just jumping in and going nuts. If you don't plan and organize your search you will be frustrated and disappointed sooner rather than later. You will feel like you are making no headway and that you are barely treading water. Take the time to map out all the different parts of the search process. We will take them one-by-one to help you put it all together.

You don't know where you are going unless you know where you've been.

It may seem trite but it is true. Unless you take a good cold hard look at where you have been and how you got to where you are now, it will be tough to figure out where you are going. This is the period of reflection and review of your career to date, its high and low points.

A couple of things to ask yourself as you go through this process are "What do I do best?" and, if you could do it over, "What would I do differently?"

Where are you in your career? It makes a big difference as to how you approach your search. Are you young and looking for the best way to climb the corporate ladder? Are you fresh out of college and looking for your first job? Are you at the other end of your career and need something that will give you employment for the last five years of your career? Has the thought of working for yourself been bouncing around inside your head for a while?

This is the time to dream a bit. What have you always wanted to do? Be a senior executive? Write? Paint? Build boats? Race cars? Help children or seniors? Teach? Homemaker? Sex therapist? In business for yourself? Don't limit yourself because you really can do anything. You just have to believe in yourself. Most people are what they believe themselves to be.

Once you envision that ideal position, honestly consider the skills and experience necessary to be successful. Personal capabilities and comparable experience certainly can open new doors. However, for any position, carefully identify the skills, training, traits, and abilities that are needed for success. If your analysis leaves you uncertain, or worse fretful, about a position then pursue other options or put it aside until you have concrete, identifiable reasons for pursuing. The sage approach is to analyze your skills and traits versus the dream position so that you first know that you can succeed and then are positioned to convince an employer. Alternatively, and not as standard practice, you may choose to shoot for the moon and pursue a dream position. This is one time in your life when you have nothing to lose by pursuing the occasional, rare, highly prized opportunity. So push forward and give that dream the potential for life.

Financial:

One of the most important factors is what the job pays. In your evaluation of an offer, you should include the dollar cost of the benefits you will receive. Generally, the cost of benefits on a per employee basis is between 30-35% of the salary. So, for example, if the job pays $50,000 but there is a good health plan, a retirement plan, short and long term disability, and life insurance, then the total compensation, assuming cost of benefits is 35%, is $67,500. If you are offered a position that also pays $50,000 but only has a health plan as a benefit then the total compensation will be less. While this is not rocket science, it is another factor to consider in your job search. In determining the needed compensation, you must factor in enough to cover your living expenses including rent/mortgage, food, transportation, utilities, clothing, entertainment, etc.

The Commute:

How far are you willing to commute? Commuting into the major metropolitan areas can take hours each way. It is not unusual for people working in those areas to have a two-hour or more round-trip commute each day.

That leads into the quality of life issue. What are you willing to give up for a job, perhaps the dream job? Are you willing to spend up to twenty hours a week in a car, van, or train? I knew one weary fellow employee who, every day, took her car to a meeting spot and then commuted across two states by van to a train and then boat before walking the last blocks to work. Not many of us would tolerate that punishing routine for long.

How much time do you want to have outside of the job to pursue your interests whatever they may be? This may be one of the most difficult decisions in the entire search process. You may decide your family is more important than the ideal job or career so you are willing to accept a position closer to home for a lesser salary than a longer commute and more money, if that means you will have less time with your loved ones or to pursue activities that are important to you. Everyone is different and certain things are more important to you at the various stages of your life.

Telecommuting, otherwise known as working from home, may be an option but one that should be considered carefully. Many jobs don't offer that option but for those that do, it can be good. Not only can you be (notice I did not say you are) more productive, but you can be on a conference call in your pajamas. No one ever said you can't enjoy yourself when working.

Like everything else, there is a good and a bad side to working from home. You lose the daily contact with your fellow workers. Now, some of you may say that you would not mind seeing your fellow employees less often, but take it from someone who has been there, it does make a difference. If you work from home often, you can get out of the loop. It is also easy to fool yourself into thinking you will be more productive. That may not be the case. Realizing that yes, you can get out of bed a half-hour before you start working and, if you don't have a meeting until mid-morning, the temptation is there to sleep in a bit, just today.

13

If you stick to a regular schedule, just like you would if you went into the office every day, you will find yourself more productive than you would if you don't have a regular schedule.

It is very true that the flexibility working from home provides is good but it can be a curse as well as a blessing depending on your particular situation and amount of self-discipline.

How much stress will you accept?

When you have been out of work for a while and you really need a job, this may be a lesser consideration although it is still an important one. Working in a job that has a continually high stress level may not be what you want or need at whatever stage of life you are in. This is a personal decision and everyone is willing to accept different work conditions. Some people thrive on stress, others want as little of it as possible. Just another thing for you to consider in evaluating what you want from your career.

You may be reading this thinking I am full of crap because you need a job, any job, and will take one regardless of the amount of stress. In that case, you are looking for a paycheck not a career. That is not a bad thing at all. Sometimes a job you take just to make ends meet turns into a satisfying and rewarding career choice.

Potential satisfaction:

You will have an interview that excites you. You know you will be able to do a good job and contribute to the organization's success. It just feels right. The planets are aligning in your favor and it seems like this will be the one. When you enter a new position feeling that way, you have a greater likelihood of success than if you are taking a job just because it is a job.

Researching occupations:

If you are interested in finding out more about various occupations, the Bureau of Labor Statistics Occupational Outlook, www.bls.gov/ooh, is a great source of information. It provides a description of the position, the future need for that type of position, compensation range, and educational requirements.

In finding a new job, you need to make a sale. You are selling your skills, knowledge, and abilities. In order to be successful, you must follow the sales process of prospecting, getting in the door, and closing the sale. Each of these can be a considerable effort.

There are three ways to execute a job search. One is to get in touch with all of your contacts to ask about whom they know and what positions may be available. Another is to apply for every job that interests you. This is a shotgun approach where you figure that it is a numbers game—the more jobs you apply for the greater your chances of success. The last is a combination of the two, what I call a targeted approach.

The targeted approach is where you identify a job, most likely through a job alert. You then go to LinkedIn, www.linkedin.com, and review your contacts to see who does, or did, work there. You may find a former colleague that has a connection at the company. If that is the case, ask for an introduction. If someone you know works there, send them an email that includes the job description and ask if they know anyone in the area or department in which the position is open. If they don't, then apply online and hope for the best. If they do know someone, ask for an immediate referral because time counts. Contact this person and let them know the position you are applying for, your qualifications, and interest in working there. Ask what they know of the position, hiring manager, and department. Try to get as much information as possible. Most likely, they will ask you to send them your resume so they can forward it to either the hiring manager or human resources or sometimes both. After this conversation or email, apply online. Use whatever information you where able to get to customize your resume and cover letter. For instance, if the person you contact says that they know the hiring manager is looking for someone with experience in a particular area, and you have that experience, craft your resume and cover letter to highlight that.

In order to conduct a productive search campaign, focus your efforts on pursuing multiple tasks and opportunities at the same time, i.e., actively seeking new opportunities through networking and online, tracking submitted applications, preparing applications, cover letters and resumes, having first and second interviews, writing thank you letters, and first and second interview follow ups. If you do this, then you won't be placing all your energy and expectations into only one position at a time. If you apply for one job at a time, and have no other activity, it can take you forever to land a new job because, if you go through the entire process and don't get the job, you have taken two steps back and must start all over again

The most crucial element in a successful job search is time management. If you cannot organize and schedule your time you will have difficulty finding a job in a reasonable timeframe.

Distraction and procrastination are the two biggest issues. They go hand-in-hand, as distraction can lead to procrastination. You may find yourself rationalizing the time you took away from your job search and that is only natural. The problem is when you are spending more time on things other than your search.

It is very easy to get distracted. This could include a quick run to the store, the phone call or texting with friends, relatives, former co-workers, cruising the Internet, checking out Facebook, or doing more research on a topic that it only slightly relevant to your task. There are many ways to get distracted and you must recognize it when it happens. Once you get distracted, you may justify it by saying "I'll do that job search thing this afternoon." Well, the afternoon becomes tomorrow morning which becomes tomorrow afternoon. Time has a way of slipping by quicker than we think it does. You need to maintain your focus.

Your job is finding a job and you should approach it like that. Try to keep a regular schedule. For example, be ready to go at 8:00 a.m., go through emails from 8:00-9:00, phone calls at 9:00 – 10:00, and online job applications 10:00-1:00. Factor in time to customize your resume and craft a cover letter for each job application. Take a break from 1:00-1:30 and then back at it for another two hours before quitting for the day. You will probably not be able to stick to this type of schedule each and every day as you have things going on that must be addressed such as doctor's appointments or other personal matters. Also, include in your weekly schedule to meet a couple people, former colleagues or referrals from contacts, for lunch or coffee each week to keep in touch with them and see how you may be able to help each other.

I am sure you have heard that networking is the key to any successful job search. Networking, networking, networking, over and over and over. It is true though. Keeping in contact with people is essential to a successful job search. Understand that networking is a two-way street — you need to give to get. It is helpful to meet with other folks looking for work so you can share information about different companies and contacts.

Most jobs are found not advertised. Estimates range from 70-80% of all jobs are filled through networking. Regardless of the actual number, the point is that the majority of jobs are filled by knowing someone.

Once you figure out how to best network and overcome any call reluctance you may have, you can make great contacts that are willing to assist you. Some sources for networking are fellow employees from the current and past jobs, LinkedIn, state or local career centers, college career services, and by joining industry associations and community groups and volunteering for committees in those organizations.

When networking, one point to keep in mind is that good manners are good business. Please and thank you are free and can go a long way to the success of your search. If you do not thank someone, it gives the impression you expected them to help you. That is not a good way to proceed.

If you are going to get in touch with your contacts you need to tell them what you are looking for and how they can assist you. For example, here is an email format. This can also be used for a telephone call, something we will cover in a bit.

The subject of the email should be "Looking for your assistance" or something like that. Generally, people are willing to help others. You need to ask in the right way and in such a manner that is friendly, is not an imposition, and lightly prods them.

Here's an example of an email request.

Bob,

I hope you are well and enjoying the (if you know of something specific this contact enjoys, mention it.) Hope you have enjoyed fishing/skiing/gardening/etc., this spring/ summer/ winter/ fall.

I am looking for a (type of position) in the (name of industry) in the (geographic area) and am hoping you can assist me.

Do you know anyone I can contact?

Thanks!

All the best,

A variation on that is when you have been referred by a contact to someone outside of your network. It is normal to be reluctant to contact people who you do not know, especially by telephone, because of a fear of being rejected. As in every sales process, if you do not get a response after two attempts, move on to the next one. Your time is too valuable to spend trying to contact people who have no inclination to help you.

The easiest thing to do is to add another sentence or two to the email. Something to the effect of:

Joe,

(referral name) suggested I contact you. We worked together at ABC Company for many years. For email requests, you should expect 40-50% of your contacts to respond and 50-60% of those to offer some form of assistance.

Contacting someone on the phone can be a difficult thing for many people because of the fear of personal rejection. An email generally does not express as much emotion as does a human voice. Many people do not want to call a contact or referral. The possibility of hearing a dismissive or unhelpful tone in someone's voice can be difficult to accept because you can tell they are probably not interested in helping you. On the other hand, if you do it right a phone call can be much better than an email because you get to express your enthusiasm and gratitude for their assistance. Here's a sample phone script:

Hello, Bob Jones speaking.

Bob, my name is Bill Smith. John Adams suggested I call you. John and I worked together for many years at XYZ company. Bob, the reason I am calling is that I am currently seeking a new position and John thought you might be able to assist me. Is this a good time to talk for a few minutes?

At this point they may say they are not sure they can help you but will listen to you. Or, they may say this is not a good time to talk and either ask you to contact them at another time or ask if they may call you. This can either be that they are truly busy and want to give you some of their time or it can be a blow off, trying to get you off the phone as quickly as possible. Ask if you can send them an email with your information so they can look at it when they have the time.

Assuming they are willing to talk here's how it might go:

"Sure, I have a minute or two."

"Great. Thanks. I worked in the (industry) in different positions over the years and am now looking for a (type of position) in the (geographic area). I have experience in (name areas of expertise) and am looking for people to contact."

"Well, have you tried (name or person(s)? I belong to the XYZ association and might be able to put you in touch with a few people. Send me an email and I'll see what I can do."

If a contact helps you, thank them through either an email or handwritten note. Acknowledging their consideration is vital to maintain a good connection with them. One thing you should not do is to reject assistance when offered — after all, you asked for it. Not accepting the help offered is a sure way to burn a bridge because that contact is far less likely to help you again.

In addition to thanking them for their help, if a lead turns into an interview, let them know. It is a good practice to keep them in the loop as to what is happening. If you get the position, you should thank them for all their help. If you do not thank them, they will be far less likely to help you again in the future if you need it.

Keep your eye on the news for the industry you are either working in or in which you want to work. There are always articles that provide information as to where the economy and industries are headed. For example, if you see several articles citing different sources indicating the economy is on an upward swing then you will know job prospects should improve also. These articles may also note those industries that are expanding or contracting. Many of the service industries such as hospitality usually increase in a good economy. Some of these articles point out those industries that are shrinking through company consolidation and/or layoffs. This information will give you an idea of what industries to explore or not.

There are three types of recruiters: employment agencies, niche recruiters, and executive search firms.

Recruiters work for the employer, not for you. They are tasked with finding the most qualified candidate for the position. Recruiters match their group of candidates to their clients open positions. Strong candidates are put forward for an interview with potential employers on a contract or direct basis. It is possible for an employer to work with more than one search firm to fill a position. An employer may have agreements with several firms and they will review the candidates put forth by those firms.

Employment agencies have a physical location where jobseekers go for an in-person interview and an assessment. These agencies generally operate within a limited geographic area and focus, for the most part, on non-professional jobs.

Niche recruiters specialize in one or two areas. They seek candidates with narrow experience such as physicians, or specific engineering or information technology knowledge and skills. These firms can be very effective at placing candidates with superior firms. This specialization allows them to offer more jobs in a particular area for they become well known for their specialty and may place candidates in multiple roles over their career.

Executive search firms may work within broad areas, such as financial services, the medical field, or information technology for example. These firms have many contacts and work with many companies within each industry.

Recruiters are busy and knowing how to work with them can go a long way in establishing a good relationship and demonstrating you are the best candidate for the job. Here are a few things to consider:

The accomplishments, personal qualities, and experience you have are your own. In that way you are unique — no one else brings to the party what you do. You need to present yourself — your skills, and experiences — in a way to be noticed by recruiters.

- Customize your resume and cover letter. Do not use a generic format you find on the Internet.

Recruiters see these all the time and can identify them quickly. Not customizing your materials shows a lack of interest and creativity. When responding to a recruiter's posting, craft your cover letter and resume to the requirements of the position. Not addressing an email or letter to the recruiter by name will get it tossed in the circular file. "Dear Recruiter" is not the way to start especially when the posting lists their name.

- Do not send a blast email to every recruiter you can find. If they are not a specialist in your field, the email will be deleted and you just wasted some of your valuable time.
- Recruiters are swamped with resumes from unqualified candidates. Make sure yours stands out and will get noticed.
- Do not apply for positions for which you are not qualified. Meeting only 70% of the qualifications does not work. Never has, never will. Respect the recruiter's time.

To reiterate what was said earlier, this is a business decision. If a recruiter says no, accept it. Do not call or email after you are told you are not a qualified candidate. Keep in mind that with the volume of resumes a recruiter receives, if you are not a qualified candidate, you will not hear from them; they do not have the time to contact everyone who submitted a resume. Remember, they are busy people. If you continue to call, you may burn a bridge you might need in the future.

If a recruiter tells you that you did not make the cut because there were more qualified candidates, accept it gracefully, thank them, and ask if you can touch base again in the future.

Here are a few things to keep in mind when communicating with a recruiter through email.

- Make sure your resume is in Microsoft Word format. It is the most common word processing software and is easy to use. Other types of files, such as PDF, are not as user-friendly. Do not send a URL to your LinkedIn page and request that they download your resume. The harder you make it for them to work with you the less success you will have.
- Make sure your name is in the file name. John Smith Insurance Consultant

resume.doc is much better than Insurance Consultant resume.doc. A recruiter could have many resumes with that title. Do not put anything like bestcandidate.doc since it is not easy for them to identify. Make it easy for them to find, identify, and file your resume.

- Do not write in all caps (ALL CAPS) or put emoticons such as smiley faces in an email. You are trying to present a professional appearance and those two things will definitely hurt your chances.

Overall, working with a recruiter can be a productive and enjoyable experience if done right. Much of it is common sense and good manners.

This is probably the best place to address contracting or temporary work since it requires a recruiter. A contractor is someone not employed by the company where he or she is working but is either self-employed or is an employee of the recruiting firm that placed them in the job.

The cost of an employee to an organization is much greater than that of a contractor. As mentioned before, an employee's compensation includes the cost of benefits. If there are no benefits then the cost to the employer has decreased substantially. An employer will contact a recruiter and let them know they are looking for a candidate or candidates with certain skills and experience. The recruiter then goes through their database of resumes to see who might be a match. If they do not have enough possible candidates in their own database, then they will post a listing online. They then go through the screening process for those that make the initial cut.

There is far more contracting nowadays than previously as many employers seek to reduce costs by having workers that do not require benefits.

Contractors are usually hired for projects. Sometimes, for a very large project, 100 or more people may be brought in. Most of the time, it is a few to several people.

A contract candidate's geographical location is less important than if they were being hired as an employee. It is not uncommon for contractors to come from all parts of the country. Quite often, contractors will fly in on a Sunday night, work at the employer's location until flying out Thursday night, and work from home Friday. I personally know of situations where for projects located in Massachusetts, the contractors came from Chicago, Dallas, Nashville, Little Rock, and St. Louis.

The money side of things is a bit different than getting a salary from an employer. Contractors are paid by the hour. A recruiter gets paid by taking a percentage of the hourly rate. For example, let's say an employer is willing to pay $75 an hour for a contractor. The recruiter will find someone for $50 and keep $25. It is a fair way of being compensated for their services. Many recruiters tell you what the position pays; it may be in the posting. This is the amount they will pay you. When you talk to a recruiter about a position, they will generally ask you what your hourly rate is, and if it is a W-2 or 1099 rate. That refers to whether you want to become their employee and receive an IRS form W-2, or be independent and get a 1099 income statement. The difference is that, as an employee, you may have some form of benefits, whereas as an independent contractor you have nothing but income. Any benefits you want and need, you provide yourself. Independent contractors get a higher hourly rate than employees of the recruiting firm. Also, as an employee, taxes and any government required withholdings for things such as Social Security and unemployment, are made for you. As an independent, you are self-employed and need to make those payments, generally through quarterly estimated tax payments to the IRS and the state in which you reside.

There are two types of contracting positions — temporary or temporary to permanent. If the position is temporary then it means the project is of a limited timeframe, although there is always the chance of it being extended, something that happens fairly frequently. When the project is over, the contractor is finished. A temp-to-perm situation is where the employer wants to bring someone on as a contractor with the intent of hiring them permanently. From the employer's perspective, it is a chance to 'test drive' someone before offering them the position.

Going the contracting route is a good way to get back to work. Find some positions online that you are qualified for and contact the recruiter to discuss the position and your situation. If you get on good terms with a recruiter, they may call you first when a new opportunity comes across their desk.

There are enough job search sites to boggle the mind. A Google search for job search websites turned up 192 million results. The one I have used most successfully is Indeed. It, like other sites, rolls up all the jobs from other job sites. It is a single source for all jobs. Many of the others job sites such as Monster list only those jobs posted by their subscribers. Sites such as Indeed sweep the Internet daily and will provide you with job alerts based on your criteria.

Here are links for some of the more popular ones:

http://www.indeed.com

http://www.linkedin.com

http://www.monster.com

http://www.careerbuilder.com

https://www.theladders.com

http://www.dice.com

https://www.usajobs.gov (For federal government jobs)

https://www.glassdoor.com

http://www.simplyhired.com

Set up job alerts and have emails sent daily so you know what jobs are out there. Having two or three job search alerts from three or four job search sites can quickly become overwhelming. Be selective in which you choose and be specific when determining the criteria.

The purpose of a cover letter is to get a recruiter to look at your resume. The purpose of a resume is to get a phone interview. The purpose of a phone interview is to get an in-person interview. The purpose of an in-person interview is to get a second interview. The purpose of the second interview is to get a job offer. The purpose of a job offer is to secure a new position. That's it in a nutshell. Each of the items has a specific purpose and they should be used as such.

Not all jobs require all of these steps. Some will not have a phone interview or even a second interview. Some won't require a cover letter.

Don't reinvent the wheel every time to put together a resume. Take information from previous resumes for similar jobs. Use action words such as managed, coordinated, created, succeeded, developed, expanded. Highlight your accomplishments.

Keep organized by setting up folders for every organization to which you apply. Keep the resume, cover letter, and job description in one place so you can refer to it in the future when prepping for the interview or writing a thank you letter.

Take your time. Don't rush it or you will end up with a resume and cover letter than is less than the best you can produce. That will show when someone reads it. In addition, after you send it you will, like many others, think about things you should have included that would have increased your chances of getting an interview. Write both as well as you can then walk away from them for an hour or two, then go back and review them. You will see certain things you need to change to make both perfect.

Being asked for the desired salary or salary history is always a tough question to answer. Many employers use it as a screening tool. If your desired salary falls at the top end of their range, then you are too expensive. If you state a salary below the bottom of the salary range, they will assume, rightly or wrongly, that you will take another job with a higher salary. Remember about the overall cost on an employee to an organization. The higher the salary, the higher the benefit cost.

COVER LETTER

The cover letter should be simple, direct, and persuasive. The entire point of a cover letter is to get the potential employer to read your resume.

Here's a format I've found successful. Your name is bold to attract attention.

YOUR NAME

ADDRESS

HOME PHONE NUMBER

CELL PHONE NUMBER

EMAIL ADDRESS

I saw the (name of position including job number) on the (give source of listing) and am very interested in it. The role seems like an exceptional fit for (company name/division if necessary) need and my skills and experience. I believe I would be a strong addition to the (specific department or team) for three reasons:

Add three short paragraphs here of two bullet points as to why you are qualified. As an example:

40

Sales and Marketing Support experience:

- I assisted in marketing retirement products across advisor, broker, and partner distribution channels and was actively involved in the development of plan and product specific marketing collateral.

- I provided sales and marketing training to agents and brokers, and coordinated the development of marketing and prospecting programs, presentations, and communications material to increase financial advisors sales capabilities.

I welcome the opportunity to meet with you for an interview. You can reach me at (phone number). I look forward to hearing from you!

Thank you for your time and consideration.

Sincerely,

(Your name)

Here is what it looks like in finished form:

YOUR NAME
ADDRESS
HOME PHONE NUMBER
CELL PHONE NUMBER
EMAIL ADDRESS

I saw the Sales and Marketing Program Manager on Indeed.com and am very interested in it. The role seems like an exceptional fit for ABC Marketing and Sales need and my skills and experience. I believe I would be a strong addition to the Product Marketing team for three reasons:

Sales and Marketing Support experience:

- I assisted in marketing retirement products across advisor, broker, and partner distribution channels and was actively involved in the development of plan and product specific marketing collateral.

- In my last position, I provided sales and marketing training to agents and brokers, and coordinated the development of marketing and prospecting programs, presentations, and communications material to increase financial advisors sales capabilities.

Second area of experience:

- Bullet One
- Bullet Two

Third area of experience:

- Bullet One
- Bullet Two

I welcome the opportunity to meet with you for an interview. You can reach me at 888-999-7777.

I look forward to hearing from you!

Thank you for your time and consideration.

Sincerely,

John Smith

Make sure the resume does not exceed two pages because a recruiter will scan it for fifteen to thirty seconds. It should be single spaced in twelve point Times New Roman font since it is easy to read. You do not want to use multiple font types, sizes or colors because it is distracting. A resume should be clean with lots of white space and one inch margins.

YOUR NAME

ADDRESS

HOME PHONE NUMBER

CELL PHONE NUMBER

EMAIL ADDRESS

Professional Overview

List, as bullet points, a few of those experiences that make you what you are, your general qualifications or "soft skills." For example:

- Energetic, pro-active professional with strong communication, analytical, interpersonal, and facilitation skills.
- Adept at driving strong business relationships, both internally and externally.
- Confident self-starter with excellent presentation, negotiation, and organizational skills.
- Able to work successfully with all levels of an organization.
- Confident decision-making skills and strong customer service orientation.
- Proven creative problem resolution abilities.

Professional Skills and Attributes

This section is optional. You can use it to hone in on why you are a strong candidate for the position. The idea is that the above section shows why you are a good employee while this section shows why you are specifically qualified for the position for which you are applying. For example:

- Provided leadership to achieve project and program goals and objectives.
- Management experience including hiring, training, supporting, and coaching employees.
- Developed and managed multiple successful relationships with vendors, program administrators, businesses clients including federal, state, and local governments.
- Wide ranging, hands-on experience including program and project management, relationship management, sales and sales support, agent training, and product development and distribution.

Professional Experience

The format for this section can be as follows:

Company name, city/town, state, dates of employment

Position title

Each of the positions you list should have three to five bullet points. Do not list a dozen because a recruiter will not read it all the way through. Do not list just responsibilities but include accomplishments. Be as specific as possible. For example: "Increased sales 82% over two years through development of new distribution channel."

Generally, for those who have been in the job market for some time, you want to go back no more than ten years. If you had a job more than ten years ago you think relates to the one you are applying for, a recruiter will think it is not relevant because it was too long ago.

For those folks who are new to the wonderful world of employment, list the jobs you have had as well as any college experience such as internships or volunteer programs.

Education and Training

List your education in this format:

The name of the school, city/town, state, degree earned.

Any training programs you took whether through a former employer or on your own,

should be listed here.

Here is what it looks like in finished form:

YOUR NAME
ADDRESS
HOME PHONE NUMBER
CELL PHONE NUMBER
EMAIL ADDRESS

Professional Overview

- Energetic, pro-active professional with strong communication, analytical, interpersonal, and facilitation skills.
- Adept at driving strong business relationships, both internally and externally.
- Confident self-starter with excellent presentation, negotiation, and organizational skills.
- Able to work successfully with all levels of an organization.
- Confident decision-making skills and strong customer service orientation.
- Proven creative problem resolution abilities.

Professional Skills and Attributes

- Provided leadership to achieve project and program goals and objectives.
- Management experience including hiring, training, supporting, and coaching employees.

49

- Developed and managed multiple successful relationships with vendors, program administrators, businesses clients including federal, state, and local governments.
- Wide ranging, hands-on experience including program and project management, relationship management, sales and sales support, agent training, and product development and distribution.

Professional Experience

ABC Company, Boston, MA,
August 2013-Present
Senior Program Manager
- Bullet One
- Bullet Two
- Bullet Three

XYZ Company, San Ramon, CA,
May 2009-July 2013
Program Manager
- Bullet One
- Bullet Two
- Bullet Two

LMN Company, San Francisco, CA, January 2005-May 2009
Program Coordinator
- Bullet One
- Bullet Two

Education and Training

ABC University, Worcester, MA
Bachelor of Arts

Management Institute, June 2011
Program Manager Certification

Before we jump into the application process, let's take a minute and review the entire process. As I mentioned in the introduction, hiring someone costs money, sometimes a lot of money.

There are many steps in the employer's search for the candidate. Remember, the purpose of each step in the process is to bring you to the next step. If the cover letter and resume pass the keyword screen, it gets you to a recruiter's review that then gets you a phone interview that then gets you to an in-person interview that then gets you a job offer. It is a long, involved, sometimes difficult process but something you must do if you want that particular job. Success is not just landing the job, but making it to the next step.

The manager must write, with the assistance of human resources, a complete and accurate job description. This can take time because it serves two purposes; clarifying for the company what they need and want in the person filling the position based on their current business model and operational needs, and providing the information to the candidate as to what qualifications are needed to be considered. After the job description is written, it is posted to various search engines and to the employer's website.

Once the online applications start coming in, there is a whole process, which we will get to in detail below, each step of which has an associated cost. For larger companies with human resources departments, a recruiter will be assigned to handle the hiring process for a particular job. Keep in mind that an internal recruiter can have many positions they are working on at a time so they are busy. In smaller organizations, the human resources department can be just one or two people so they do everything, in addition to other job responsibilities.

My point is to make you aware that it takes considerable time and money to hire someone. An employer wants to find the right candidate while minimizing cost. Again, this is a business process.

Here's what happens after you hit "send":

Automated keyword screen:

Since it is now so easy to apply for a job, there can be hundreds of resumes received for one position in a short period of time. In order to make the process more efficient, there are software programs that screen resumes to filter out the candidates whose resumes best match the job description. Each job description contains keywords that vary depending on the industry and position. If your resume contains enough of the keywords, it is retained. If your resume does not contain any or enough keywords it is not selected for further review. Usually, only a certain number of resumes are selected. For example, a recruiter might decide that once they have fifty candidates from the keyword search to look at only those. The rest are not considered. So even if you think you are the world's best candidate for the job, and you may well be, if you are number fifty-one, you don't make the initial cut. Nothing personal in it, it is just the way the process works.

Human review:

As the recruiter has other positions they are working on, there is not a great deal of time to spend going through each and every cover letter and resume so a recruiter at a large company may spend thirty seconds looking at each of those selected. If your resume passes the keyword screening, then the recruiter reviews it. Of the fifty people in our example, six or eight are chosen for phone interviews. If your resume matches the requirements, a phone interview is scheduled. Not all employers do phone interviews, some preferring to go right to the face-to-face interview but in my experience, many do a phone interview or screening.

Phone interview:

The best advice I can give you regarding interviews is to be yourself. Do not try to be what you think they want you to be. If you are genuine it shines through. If you are not, it is apparent and will cut short the interview.

The phone interview is important but only as the next step. A phone interview can take from ten minutes to one hour depending on the amount of information the recruiter needs to make a decision as to whether to bring you in for an in-person interview. Sometimes the hiring manager may want to do a phone interview with you after the recruiter has spoken with you.

You've made it to the in-person interview stage. Great! The employer sees something about your skills and experiences that make them want to discuss the role and your qualifications. That is a good thing but it can be a nerve-wracking experience especially for those that have not been in such an interview in a long time, if ever. This is the next to last step in the hiring process and is your chance to shine, to let the employer know that you are the right person for that job.

Now, let's look at preparing for the interview.

The first thing you must do is to know your resume inside and out. This may sound obvious but to many people it isn't. A recruiter will ask different types of questions about various positions or responsibilities you've held and if you stumble over an answer, or don't seem to be able to accurately relate your experience to the question, you probably will not advance to the next step. You must also understand the job description. Read it over several times, relate it to your past jobs, and think about how you can meet the requirements. When developing your responses to potential questions, it may help to write them down.

One of the best ways of prepping for an interview is to learn as much as you can about the organization and the people you will be speaking with and to concentrate on your qualifications for the job. Ask who you will be meeting with. Some organizations will send an email with the times of the meetings and the name and position of the person(s) you will be meeting with. If they don't just ask; they should not have a problem telling you.

While it is a well-worn expression, it is true that you only get one chance to make a good first impression. The way you look and act counts so if you dress and act professionally you will rise above the competition. For men, a dark suit with a white or blue shirt and colorful but conservative tie will make a good impression. Make sure your shoes are shined. A giveaway as to how well you prepare is whether your shoes are shined or not. If you are dressed in a great looking suit, crisp shirt, and nice tie but your shoes are scuffed and dull, it takes away from the entire look. It says that you did not care enough about the interview to give it your all.

Do not wear lots of jewelry or perfume or cologne. If a woman wears many bracelets, it can be distracting especially if she keeps jangling them. That will annoy the interviewer. Likewise, if you wear perfume or cologne, you risk offending the interviewer because of the smell. Some people are sensitive to strong odors and it becomes a true distraction.

For women, a nice, conservative suit or jacket or blouse, skirt or slacks, or dress is fine. No loud colors or prints, no short skirts or super high heels, nothing that might be offensive. Remember, you are seeking a new job not having a social encounter. Do not scuttle your chance at a job by under dressing. Your first goal is to make a good impression. You need to look clean-cut. Many interviews end prematurely because of a candidate's improper dress and annoying actions. Wearing a suit for an interview at an organization where employees wear jeans, T-shirts, and flip flops will make you stand out but it is better to be overdressed than underdressed.

Do not, I repeat do not, under any circumstances, take out your phone during the interview. Turn it off and put it in a pocket or purse. If you check your phone during the interview, it is almost a guarantee that you are no longer a candidate. The interviewer will find it rude and unprofessional. So long job!

Not all interviewers are good interviewers. Like many things in life, some are better than others. There may be just one interviewer or possibly more. Gang or panel interviews — where a few to several people interview you at the same time — are not uncommon.

The interviewer will ask you questions and they can be of two types: functional — relating to your past career experiences, or behavioral — how did or would you do something.

Some typical questions:

▪ Tell me about yourself.

The answer to this question can be an interview killer. The interviewer is not looking for your life story but how your experience relates the position qualifications. Tell them what you have done successfully in the past that can be applied to this position.

▪ What have you been doing lately?

If you have been out of work, explain how that came about and what you have been doing. Do not say "Looking for a job." That is understood. That is why you are there. They want to know how you are keeping your skills and knowledge up-to-date. If there is a gap in your resume, explain it. Perhaps it was a family or personal medical situation. Let them know but do not go into detail. A one sentence answer is fine.

- What are the best skills you bring to the position?
- How would you do (something?)
- Tell me about a time when…
- Why should we hire you?

Keep your answers short and to the point, no more than two minutes each. Do not wander or ramble as it will cause the interviewer to lose interest in you. Look the interviewer in the eye when answering but do not stare as that will make them uncomfortable.

If the interviewer asks what compensation you want do not answer it with a number. If you do, you will lock yourself in and that may be a big disadvantage. The best way to deal with it is to ask what the salary range of the position. Usually, the interviewer will give a general answer, "$50,000 to $70,000." You then know where to place yourself in that range. "The upper third of that range is appropriate for my skills and experience," is a good response.

When you are done answering their questions and they have answered yours, summarize why you are the best candidate for the position. Review your past accomplishments, skills, and work ethic, and how you are the person they are looking for in the role. Remember, now is the time to close the sale.

To be good you must practice. Would you go onstage to make a presentation or play an instrument before practicing? No. Well, it is the same here.

One thing you must realize is that the organization will most likely check your online presence including social media, and run a credit check on you. The reason for looking at these two items are that they want to assure themselves that you are a responsible, reliable person. If you posted many photos of you and your buddies out drinking and partying, or put up pictures of your or someone else's various body parts, for example, it will not be well received. If you have made questionable posts that include pornography, comments that are racist, intolerant of other peoples and religions, or show you to be something other than what you represent yourself to be, it will greatly diminish your chance for success in the search process. The point is to be careful of what you post. If there are things you wouldn't show to your mother, take them down. Otherwise, change your privacy settings so posts do not appear in a search.

Likewise, a potential employer looks at an applicant's credit report to see if they have handled their finances in a responsible manner. If you have a poor credit score due to paying all your bills late or not paying them at all, it will pretty much nix your chances. When you go for an interview, you will be asked to complete an application and sign a form allowing the potential employer to check your credit. If you decline to sign the form, it is a tip off that you believe your score is poor.

INTERVIEW QUESTIONS

There are many questions to ask during an interview but you want to focus on those that give you the greatest amount of information and insight into the company and manager. You need to gather this information to decide whether it is the right company and position for you. Be aware that you have some control over the interview. It should be a back-and-forth discussion not an interrogation by the interviewer. Don't hesitate to ask a question. Remember, you need to decide if you want to work for them.

Below are just some examples of questions. Try not to use standard questions, i.e., those you pull off the Internet because recruiters and managers have seen and heard most of them. Try to be a bit original.

The first question you should ask is about what qualities they are looking for in a candidate because it will tell you how to relate your qualifications and experience to what they are looking for.

The second question, inquiring about the culture and spirit of the company, will give you insight into the type of company it is. That information will help you position yourself in the best light possible.

Before you head to the interview, type the list of questions you want to ask. Bring a pen, a notebook, or a folder with a pad of paper with you. When you sit down with the interviewer take your list of questions out and put them on the table. Right up front, mention that you have questions you want to ask so they know. Here are some to consider asking:

- What are the top three/four qualities are you looking for in the person filling this role?
- How would you describe the culture or spirit in this company?
- What types of people tend to excel here?
- Can you tell me a little more about the current situation? Why is the position open?
- What is a typical day in the job?
- Can you tell me about the way the job has been performed in the past? What improvements would you like to see happen?

- What are the challenges and priorities I would face in this position over the next three months?
- Can you give me an example of each of the responsibilities?
- How does this person interact with other employees in the department?
- What is the reporting/organizational structure?
- How would you describe your management style and interaction with your staff?
- How does the department interact with other departments?
- What level of experience do the employees in this area have?
- How will my responsibilities and performance be measured?
- Where are you in the hiring process?
- What do you like best about working here?

A thank you letter should be sent within twenty-four hours of the interview. Hiring managers are impressed with a good thank you letter as it shows you care enough about the job to take the time to write one which not all candidates do. Like the cover letter and resume, a thank you letter must be clear, direct, and persuasive. Do not reiterate everything you discussed in the interview. Thank the person for meeting with you, summarize your qualifications, and close with a friendly tone.

During the interview the answer to your question about where they are in the interview process will determine whether to send a hand-written card, typed letter, or an email. If the interviewer tells you they are making a decision within the next few days, an email is the timeliest method to use. If a decision is a couple of weeks away, then a mailed letter or note is best.

This is an example of a possible format and content.

YOUR NAME

ADDRESS

PHONE NUMBER

EMAIL ADDRESS

Date

Jane,

It was great meeting with you. I enjoyed our discussion about (add one or two things you talked about.)

Being an integral part of the effort to (add topic), as I mentioned, is very interesting to me. I know, with my experience and skills, I could assist in (add information specifically related to interview).

As you can tell, I am excited about the possibility of working at the (company name.)

Thanks you for your time and consideration.

All the best,

(Your name)

REFERENCES

References should be short and sweet. Include the person's name, position, company, address, phone number, and email. Most employers ask for three references. Make sure these people know you are using them as references. Get their permission beforehand. Also, they should be professional references not your Uncle Joe or cousin Billy. Here is a simple format to use if you want.

YOUR NAME

ADDRESS

PHONE NUMBER

EMAIL ADDRESS

John Smith

Field Vice President

ABC Financial Services Co.

17 Anywhere Square

Any city, Any state, zip code

Phone number

Email address

Depending on the type of position and level in the organization, the job offer can be a simple acceptance of the terms offered or negotiations that can be lengthy and complex. For some people, depending on their situation, it is a matter of saying "yes" to what is offered. Other times, it can involve some back and forth especially for a higher compensation and benefits package.

When an offer is made, it is best to take some time, anywhere from a couple of hours to a few days, depending on the level of the position, salary, benefits, and your personal situation. When the offer is made, ask the prospective employer if you can get back to them in a day or two. Sometimes they will need a decision soon because they may want to offer the position to someone else if you decline it. A prospective employer can revoke the offer at any time.

To negotiate successfully, you must know the current salary range for that type of occupation in that industry in that geographic area. If you don't and just wing it, you could seriously handicap yourself by accepting a salary lower than the prevailing wage. When asking for a higher salary, it is best to present your request in the context of your research. Something such as: *Based on my research, the current salary range for this position within the XYZ industry in this area is $xx, xxx. While the position is excellent and will allow me to contribute to the company's success and the company offers very good benefits, the only thing keeping me from accepting the offer is the salary.* The worst thing they can say is "no." Negotiating a counter offer can be tricky. If you really need the job, the inclination is to take the offer as long as it is reasonable.

After all the searching for a good position, the resume preparation, and the phone and in-person interviews, not getting a job that you want and know you are fully qualified for can be difficult, especially when you know you are one of the two or three finalists. When you see the email that usually begins *Thank you for considering employment with* or *As you know, there were a number of impressive candidates who applied for this position resulting in a very competitive interview process and we have narrowed our search to those candidates whose experience more closely fits our needs.* Yeah, yeah, yeah. You take a deep breath, wonder how a company can be so dumb as to not hire you, call them a few choice names, take another deep breath, and go on.

In this situation, ask yourself two very constructive questions: What did I do best? What will I do differently next time? Write down the answers. It will also give you a clearer picture of the things you are doing well and those that you need to improve on. For example, if one of the things you

71

need to do differently is smile more and you note more than once, then you know it is a weak point and what you need to do to correct it.

Something else to keep in mind is that second guessing everything will drive you nuts. Did I say the wrong thing? I forgot to tell them this. One of the interviewers did not seem to like me. Why? What did I do wrong? I should have worn my other suit/shoes/tie. What was I thinking? This type of self-interrogation is not productive and will generally cause you unnecessary anxiety.

The best thing you can do is to never stop networking.

Believe in yourself. You will get a job eventually. You will.

You landed a great job. You are very happy to be back to work. You feel good about contributing to your family's financial health. You have learned a great deal. However, there is always the possibility that the job may not work out. Generally, the last person in the door is the first one out. While you are tired of looking for a job, keep your eye on the job search alerts — don't cancel them yet. Give it three months in the new position. By then you will know if it will work out.

You can't do it alone.

You will find times when you need to talk with someone about what you are doing, whether it is right or wrong, whether you should even continue in your search, whether any of it makes sense.

To make sure you are able to get through the search process and survive mentally and emotionally, surround yourself with people who will support you. While it is easy to complain, do not get together with negative people for they will draw you down and make it even more difficult than it already is. Sometimes just a few words of encouragement are enough to keep you moving forward or at least prevent you from stopping in your tracks.

How you approach this depends on the type of person you are. Some people do not want to talk about their job search activities because they think it may jinx their chances, get their hopes up, or that people will be bored with their stories about how hard they are looking for a position. Other people like to talk openly about everything they are doing; it is a form of release. It that's how they keep their spirits up. Do whatever gets you through it and makes you feel better.

Considering working for yourself is daunting. You are unsure if it is the right thing to do. You worry about the effect it will have on your family and friends. You can't stop thinking about the loss of income. You fear failing, having to hang your head in shame and go back to being an employee again. It will cause you a few sleepless nights. Whether you want to work for an employer or yourself is something only you can determine. Although when someone asks what you do for a living and you tell them you are following your passion, you will hear comments like "Oh, I wish I could do that," "You're so lucky," "It must be great waking up in the morning looking forward to doing what you do." Yes, it is!

One question you need to address is your passion. What one thing are you passionate about? Do you have anything you are passionate about? If you do, great. If you don't, that's okay because not everyone does. If there is something you are doing that you really want to do for a living, and then do it.

When you are thinking of pursuing your passion or hobby as a business, you must determine what income level you will accept. It is entirely possible, and most likely probable, that you may not see any substantial income for a year, possibly longer. Many people are willing to accept a smaller income than they could otherwise earn for the happiness and enjoyment doing what they love brings them.

However, there are ways to approach it that make your success more possible. First, learn all you can about doing whatever you have in mind as a business. Maybe you've been enjoying a hobby for many years and decided you want to do that full time. Maybe you have a hidden passion that has been slowly making its way toward a realization that you can do it. Maybe you are just tired of the rat race, want to chuck it all and do something adventurous. Before you tell your boss you are leaving, do your homework. Go to the library and get books, or look online, on what you want to do. There are many books from people who've made the great leap of faith and are willing to share all they know to help people like you.

My words of wisdom here are: 1) Read all you
can about starting your own business specifically in
your field of interest, 2) Plan for a difficult start-up
period when income will be less than you were
making, 3) Realize there are many people who want
you to succeed.

You need to consider many of the same things
mentioned in the Assessing Your Needs section.
How much money do you need? Can you get by
with less? Are you willing to make the sacrifice
needed to be successful? Do you have discipline and
good time management skills? Are you willing to
work harder and smarter for yourself than you are
for an employer?

Whatever your reasons for considering working
for yourself, you will need to address the obstacles
to being successful, whatever that means to you.

When I was considering becoming a freelance
writer and editor, I read Paulo Coelho's *The
Alchemist*. It is a story, a fable really, about a boy
who is in search of his calling. It was very helpful to
me, giving me things to think about and consider in
making my decision. In the introduction, he
mentions the four obstacles to achieving your

"Personal Legend," his term for what you want and are meant to do. The obstacles are:

- We are told that we cannot do it. It takes courage to dig deep and believe in ourselves, to know that you can achieve whatever you want to do.
- We are afraid of hurting those around us by abandoning everything to pursue our dream. We need to realize that those who love us want us to succeed and will join us on our voyage of discovery.
- Fear of defeat. We are afraid of the failures and setbacks we will have to endure. We want only continual success.
- Fear of realizing our dream. When you have gotten through the first three obstacles and your dream is within your reach, you believe you are not worthy of it and turn away.

Here are a few "do's" and "don'ts" to consider when making the decision.

Do:

- Have a plan. Think it through for it will be one of the biggest decisions of your life. Figure out all the aspects of working for yourself, write a list to keep organized, spend time writing a comprehensive plan.

- Talk to others who do what you want to do. Most people are happy and secure in their self-employed professions and will share their knowledge with you.

- Find an organization or agency that can help you with you planning such as SCORE, https://www.score.org, a volunteer organizations of retired business people with the goal of mentoring and educating small business owners, the Small Business Administration, https://www.sba.gov, the local Chamber of Commerce and community development organizations. They all have resources to help you start and succeed in your pursuit of your dream.

Don't:

- Let people steal your time. Just say "no" to family and friends who think that you have all the time in the world to do whatever they ask or want you to do. Explain to them that you are working, that you need to be productive to make money, and that you can't spend the afternoon with them. However, you will always need to attend to personal matters such as medical appointments, sick children, and emergencies of one sort or another.

- Spend time on Facebook when you need to be working.
- Cruise the Internet.
- Text friends.
- Play video games.
- Slack off.

CONCLUSION

Okay, now that you have all this information, get off your butt and get a job, or figure out if you want to work for yourself. Only kidding folks. Well, I am and I am not. Use the information you gained from this, whether it was a little or a lot, to advance, and hopefully improve, your occupational situation. Knowing something is great but using it effectively is even better.

I hope I've been able to provide useful information to you. Again, it is all based on my experience, which is different from yours. But, the process has the same components and I tried to make you aware of what those are and to clarify any part of the process you may have been unclear about.

Best of luck in your future endeavors whatever they may be.

There are more job resources available to you than you will ever have time to look at. Thousands and thousands of books have been written about every aspect of the job search process. A Google search for "job search resources" returned 342 million hits. You get the idea.

Try to narrow your resource search as much as possible. It is possible to spend valuable hours looking for resources that you may never use. Take a look through the above link to see what might be applicable to your situation.

Note that I do not endorse any particular or specific website or resource. These are just examples of how best to learn about, and execute, a successful job search.

Here are some resources that you may find useful, interesting, and possibly entertaining:

Mrs. Doubtfire Job Interview
(https://www.youtube.com/watch?v=GrpWsSIXJ1I)

A novel way of interviewing for a job. This probably will not work in a real job search. Remember, anything is possible in the movies.

Job Interviews gone wrong
(https://www.youtube.com/watch?v=Gww2vrIhjeU)
A video of what not to do. These are all dramatizations but they get the point across.

41 Job Interview Questions and Answers
(https://www.youtube.com/watch?v=bLdb9_TITSw)
This is a good, informative video but it is over an hour long. However, it may be a good investment in your time.

Public libraries

Public libraries are a wonderful but often an overlooked resource. Many have industry journals and magazines, both in print and online, that will give you good background on an industry and possibly the company to which you are applying.

No one can write a book alone so special thanks to Van Leichter, Martin Dyer, Greg Jackman, and my wife Barbara for their review, comments and support.